Charles Hawkes Todd

The Irish Church

its disestablishment and disendowment

Charles Hawkes Todd

The Irish Church
its disestablishment and disendowment

ISBN/EAN: 9783744741231

Printed in Europe, USA, Canada, Australia, Japan

Cover: Foto ©Lupo / pixelio.de

More available books at **www.hansebooks.com**

THE IRISH CHURCH;

ITS DISESTABLISHMENT AND

DISENDOWMENT.

By CHARLES H. TODD, Esq., LL.D.

ONE OF HER MAJESTY'S COUNSEL, AND VICAR-GENERAL OF THE DIOCESES OF DERRY
AND RAPHOE.

London,
RIVINGTONS, WATERLOO PLACE;

HIGH STREET, | TRINITY STREET,
Oxford. | Cambridge.

1869.

THE IRISH CHURCH;

ITS DISESTABLISHMENT AND DISENDOWMENT.

THE verdict of the United Kingdom, so far as it can be conjectured from the result of the recent elections, has been recorded against the present Ecclesiastical constitution of Ireland. It still remains to be seen to what extent the country is willing to adopt the scheme shadowed forth in the Resolutions moved by Mr. Gladstone, and adopted by a large majority of the late Parliament. No one, however, be his political or religious opinions what they may, can deny the vast importance of the subject, or that legislation in the direction proposed will effect a great revolution in the constitution of these kingdoms, as regards the Country, the Crown, and the Church; a revolution whose effects cannot be confined within the shores of Ireland or of the United Kingdom, but will probably affect the relations which now exist between the Church and the civil power throughout Christian Europe.

That such a scheme should be adopted in the British Parliament by a majority of sixty, notwithstanding the gross injustice and the violation of the rights of pro-

perty involved, that it should be favourably received,
not merely by those who on religious grounds are
opposed to the reformed Church or to religious endowments of any kind, but by men of no revolutionary turn
of mind, themselves members of that Reformed Church,
is no small matter of surprise. When the component
parts of that majority which assented to Mr. Gladstone's Resolutions are analyzed, and it is found to
consist, not merely of Roman Catholics, Radicals, and
the personal followers of Mr. Gladstone, but even
partly of Conservatives, it is impossible to ascribe its
success solely to a party move to displace Mr. Disraeli's
administration. I cannot think, that were the question calmly considered and rightly understood, it could
be favourably received by any man, who values, not
merely the principles of the Reformation, but the great
principles of moral right and justice, and who respects
those rights of property which are the basis of our
great and free constitution. That the chief organ of
public opinion in England (the " Times "), that such
men as Earl Grey, Lord Russell, and Mr. Gladstone,
that the great Whig party in England, who have
hitherto so strenuously opposed all penal legislation,
should be the active promoters and supporters of such
a scheme, and put it forward as an act of justice to
any portion of the community, can only proceed from
some great misapprehension of the subject.

The argument which appears to have most weight
with the supporters of this movement, which is most
persistently put forward, is this : That it is an anomaly
that all the religious endowments of the country should
be engrossed by one religious denomination, and that
one which embraces but a small minority of the popu-

lation. This argument rests upon a palpable fallacy. It assumes that there exists in the country an endowment for general religious purposes, granted by the State, to a share of which all religious bodies are entitled, but which has been unjustly or wrongfully engrossed by one denomination, and that a minority of the people. There is no anomaly in the wealthy owners of property, although a small minority, endowing their own Church; nor is there any anomaly in a religious community, however small, acquiring property to any extent. The alleged anomaly consists in the assumption that this property was a State endowment for general religious purposes. It is also assumed, and chiefly by foreigners and persons unacquainted with this country, that in Ireland the majority of the people are taxed or in some way compelled to contribute to the maintenance of the Church of the minority; and this was actually put forward by Dr. Corrigan as an injustice, in his late address to electors of the city of Dublin. Both these assumptions, however, are untrue. The Irish Church possesses no State endowments, it derives no portion of her property from the State; neither does any dissenter from the Church in Ireland, be he Protestant or Roman Catholic, contribute one farthing to the maintenance and support of the Church or of its Clergy: Church-rates, minister's money, and all general assessments, for religious purposes, have been, in deference to the religious feelings of Roman Catholics and Protestant Dissenters, long since abolished. In Ireland, the churches, the Bishops, the Clergy, the See and glebe houses are built, maintained, and supported exclusively out of the property of the Church itself, aided by the voluntary contributions of its

own members. The only religious bodies in Ireland
who are in possession of State endowments are the
Presbyterians, who receive the *Regium Donum*, and
the Roman Catholics, who receive some 30,000*l.* or
40,000*l.* a year for the exclusive education of their
clergy. The Church of Ireland receives nothing from
the State, she is supported altogether by her own
property and the voluntary gifts of her own people.
All other religious bodies in Ireland are possessed of
property. Where, then, is the anomaly in the Irish
Church having property ? or why is its property alone
to be confiscated ?

Mr. Gladstone's Resolutions embraced two distinct
and separate matters,—Disestablishment and Disendowment; which rest on totally different principles,
and raise perfectly distinct considerations.

Disestablishment is purely a question of State policy :
it is a question more for the State than for the Church.
Nevertheless it is a very grave matter, effecting a
most serious change in the established constitution,
which has been the source of such great blessings to
these kingdoms ; and, it may be, that the State by
adopting it incurs a very great responsibility. It is not
the substitution of one form of Christianity for another ;
it is not the State declaring that the present Church
of Ireland is false in her teaching, or distasteful to the
majority of the people, and substituting for it another
system, either deemed more true or more consonant
to the feelings of the people ; but it is a rejection by
the State of ALL religion.

The union between the Church and the State is not
the result of any compact or agreement. The State
never formally recognized or adopted the Church by

any Act of Parliament.   But the ruling Powers in the country being converted to Christianity, the State submitted herself to the Church, recognized the authority of its rulers, conformed her laws to its teaching, and aided the Ecclesiastical authority by her co-active power.   The Church has received from her Divine Master no power or authority to inflict temporal pains or penalties, to her has been committed the power of the keys, not of the sword ; she can only bind or loose, admit or exclude ; she can enforce her discipline only by penance or excommunication.   The State, embracing Christianity, gave additional sanction to the laws of the Church by imposing temporal pains and penalties for the infraction of them, and gained reverence and respect for her rulers and teachers by conferring on them civil rank and status.   In England, the chief officers of the Church were also the chief officers of the State.   The Bishops administered the •law ; the assembly of the Bishops and Clergy, with the Barons and Knights, framed the laws.   By degrees Ecclesiastics were supplanted in civil matters by the laity, and were confined exclusively to Ecclesiastical and religious affairs ; so much so, that, at the present day, it would be considered inconsistent with the sacred character of a Bishop or Priest to sit as a judge in a temporal court, or to go as ambassador on a foreign mission. Still the Bishops retained their civil status ; they held courts and exercised jurisdiction, not only over the Clergy, but over laymen, and not only in matters which may be considered exclusively spiritual, but in many temporal matters, such as testamentary, matrimonial, and other causes.   But at the present day, when the principle of Religious Toleration is established,

at least in the British Empire—when it is no longer
necessary that the chief public officers and magistrates
should be members of the Church, or even Christians,
when the Ecclesiastical courts have been deprived of
almost all jurisdiction, except over the Clergy—the
Church is being regarded, more and more every day,
in the same light as any of the numerous religious
communities which exist in the country, differing from
the others, so far as regards its relation to the State,
only in this, that the Crown is the Supreme Ordinary,
her Bishops are spiritual Peers, and as such entitled
to civil rank and precedence, the law of the Church is
a part of the law of the land, the Bishops by virtue
of their office exercise jurisdiction; and the doctrines
and discipline of the Church cannot be changed without the sanction of the State. Every citizen of the
State also enjoys certain rights and privileges in the
Church, whether he conforms to her teaching and
discipline or not. All religious communities may in
these countries acquire and hold property, and that
even with less restriction than the Church, which
cannot acquire real estate without a licence in mort-
main. The rulers of these religious bodies, be they
Bishops, Presbyters, Elders, or whatever the ruling
power may be called, can exercise jurisdiction, and
expel from their society those who contravene its
teaching or oppose its discipline, and thus enforce
uniformity in practice and opinion more easily than can
the Church, because unless some civil right of property is
affected their decisions cannot be controlled by the law
of the State; whereas in the National or Established
Church, as it is called, every person has certain rights
and privileges which may be enforced in the civil

courts, and ,of which he cannot be deprived without
the sanction of the civil law. In these matters consists
the difference between the established religion and any
other religious community in the country. To disestablish the Church is to destroy this difference, to
deprive it of its privileges and advantages ; but at the
same time to relieve it from all interference and
control of the State.

How is this separation from the State, this isolation
and independence, to be effected in the case of an
institution which has grown with the State, and is so
interwoven with it, that it seems almost impossible to
rend them asunder without doing injury to one or
other, or to both ? I do not notice the difficulty said to
arise from the Act of Union between Great Britain and
Ireland. It is as competent for the Parliament to
repeal that Act as it is any other Act in the Statute
Book ; and if Mr. Gladstone recognizes " the voice of
God, in the deep, prevalent, and lasting convictions of a
people," if such convictions " are never found and
never stand the test of time and circumstances without containing in themselves much of the truth and
sacredness of justice," no measure is more imperatively
called for than the repeal of the legislative union
between these two countries, upon no subject have the
convictions of the great bulk of the population of
Ireland been more deep, prevalent, and lasting. Nor
do I press the objection which may be derived from
the constitutional law, viz. that the Clergy are one
of the estates of the realm, and that it is incompetent
for the other two states—the Lords and the Commons
—to abolish the third ; not only because I believe no
argument based on constitutional law would have any

influence on the statesmen who have embarked in this enterprise, but because the power of the Parliament to abolish the Church and adopt any other form of religion cannot be denied.

In any measure for the disestablishment of the Church, the first matter to be dealt with is the Royal Prerogative. Since the days of William the Conqueror, the right to create Bishoprics in England and to nominate Bishops thereto, has been one of the pre-rogatives of our kings,—the brightest gem in their crown, one most jealously and successfully guarded from the attempts of the Popes of Rome to usurp it. Is the Crown tamely to surrender this right to the Pope ? The Royal Supremacy is not a new dogma of the Reformation, it is one of the ancient rights of the Crown, more jealously asserted before the Reformation, when our sovereigns were Roman Catholics, than it is even now. That it is the right and prerogative of the Crown to create Bishoprics, not only in the United Kingdom, but in all the dominions of her Majesty, is an undoubted and undisputed principle of consti-tutional law, and no foreign power has or can have the power to do so. It was the attempt of the See of Rome to do this in England, which called forth that silly piece of legislation known as '' The Eccle-siastical Titles Act.'' By which the Whig minister, fearing to lose his popularity, and unwilling to allow so serious an encroachment on the Royal Prerogative to pass unnoticed, attacked the shadow, the harmless and inoffensive shadow, while he left the substance untouched. Even in Roman Catholic countries the Pope cannot create a Bishopric without the consent of the sovereign power. This right to create a Bishopric has been exercised by the Crown in almost all the British Colonies. No doubt has been thrown upon the validity of the patents appointing Colonial Bishops so far as they purport to create a Bishopric or to nominate a Bishop. The opinion given by the Judicial Committee of the Privy Council to her Majesty in Bishop Colenso's case is only as to the jurisdiction conferred on the Bishop, but the right and prerogative of the Crown to create the Bishopric has never been questioned. In any country in which there exists a large body of Roman Catholics, it is essential, not only for the government of the Church, but for the administration of those sacred offices which belong exclusively to the episcopal function, that there should be Roman Catholic Bishops; to these Bishops certain districts must be assigned within which they are to exercise their spiritual functions, and which may popularly be called Sees, although in this country, the right to create a See being in the Crown, they cannot be regarded as *legal* Sees. Accordingly, since the Reformation, there has existed in Ireland two sets of Bishops : one nominated by the Crown, and the other by the Pope— who are appointed by him to the same Sees as those appointed by the Crown. These Bishops have no legal jurisdiction, they have no civil *status*, and are regarded by the State only in the same light as the heads of any other religious body tolerated in the community. They assume, however, the titles of the Sees to which they are appointed, and claim to be the Bishops of those Sees to the exclusion of the Bishops nominated by the Crown. Thus there exist in Ireland two fully organized Churches, each claiming to be the

Church of Ireland, one adopting the principles of the
English Reformation, whose Bishops are nominated
by the Crown, subject to the law of the land, and
therefore enjoying a civil status and political rights
which are denied to the other, which in defiance of
the law acknowledges the supremacy of the Pope, and
owes its chief allegiance to him.   Of this latter Church
the great bulk of the peasantry of Ireland are members,
and have been always so since the Reformation, while
the gentry, professional, and mercantile classes, are in
nearly the same proportion members of the Reformed
Church.   During the last century the Roman Catholic
Church in Ireland has acquired great wealth ; it has
studded the country with large, if not handsome,
churches, and founded numerous conventual and
educational establishments.   The laity of the Church
have also risen, especially since 1829, in wealth, education, and position.   The highest offices in the State
may be, and are, filled by Roman Catholics ; the administration of the law is largely entrusted to them; our
municipal corporations are almost exclusively composed
of them ; and most of the Irish members of the House
of Commons are returned by Roman Catholic votes and
Roman Catholic influence.   Thus they are invested with
great political power and high social position, while the
social position of their Clergy has not received a corresponding improvement.   It is but natural that the
Roman Catholic laity should, under these circumstances, desire to see the social position of their
Bishops and Clergy improved.   And it is said that
they regard it as an injustice and an insult that the
Bishops and Clergy of the Reformed Church should
enjoy a civil position and status which is refused to

the Bishops and Clergy of their Church. To apply
the terms injustice and insult to such a matter is
simply a perversion of language. Insult, if any there
be, seems to be altogether on the other side. It is
offered to the Crown by the Pope presuming to invade
its prerogative by appointing Bishops to Sees within
its dominions. It is true that the establishment of
standing armies, the waning political power of the
Popes, and the separation of politics from religion,
which has deprived our Bishops of all political power,
enable the Crown to regard lightly such invasion of its
prerogative ; but there was a time when such usurpa-
tion was of political moment.

The position, however, of the Roman Catholic
Clergy in Ireland is undoubtedly anomalous. The
State has granted a large endowment and founded a
college for the exclusive education of the Clergy of the
Roman Catholic Church, but as soon as they are or-
dained and sent out into the country to discharge
those duties for which the State has educated them,
it ignores their existence. This is the real anomaly in
the Ecclesiastical condition of Ireland, and not either
the Establishment or the Endowment of the Reformed
Church. Mr. Gladstone proposes to remove it by
depriving the Crown of its prerogative, and leaving a
clear stage for the pretensions of the See of Rome.
It may, however, well be doubted whether this be the
only solution of the difficulty, or whether it would
not be possible to improve the position of the Roman
Catholic Bishops and Clergy in Ireland, without im-
pairing the royal prerogative or affecting in any way
the Established Church. There may be difficulty in
the State recognizing Cardinal Cullen as Archbishop

of Dublin, when the Crown has already appointed
Dr. Trench to that See; there may be difficulty in
acknowledging the Pope's claim to appoint Bishops;
yet such difficulties do not appear to be insurmount-
able, or to involve a greater violation of constitutional
law than the scheme suggested by Mr. Gladstone. It
is impossible to look around on the nations of Europe,
and not see that a time is approaching when some
change must take place in the relations which have
hitherto subsisted between the Church and the Civil
power; the continuance of the temporal power of the
Pope hangs on a thread; the Reformed Church in
these countries has been for some years growing
restive under State interference. It is struggling for
freedom, to be governed by its own laws, and to be
itself the sole judge of those who contravene its teaching or violate its discipline. It would seem to be the
natural consequence of the complete toleration of
different religious communities; and our colonies fur-
nish us with examples of countries enjoying all the
benefits of the English constitution, and yet having no
Established Churches. These things all point to a
change at no distant period in the relation between
the Church and State; when the Church shall exist in
the country, free and independent of State control,
making her own laws, herself judging offenders against
those laws, enforcing her own discipline, nominating
her own Bishops, and maintained and supported by
her own property and people. And if this was all
Mr. Gladstone proposed to do with the Irish Church,
it is possible he would meet with but little opposition
from its members.

In order to disestablish the Church in Ireland, it

will be necessary to make several changes in the law as it exists at present, some of which are here noticed:—

First. The right or prerogative of the Crown to create Bishoprics in Ireland, and to appoint Bishops to the Sees already existing, must be taken away. This prerogative the Crown has enjoyed in England since the reign of William the Conqueror, and in Ireland since the reign of Henry II. In England, Bishoprics were originally donative by the Crown by delivery of the ring and crozier; they were made elective in the reign of King John, and afterwards made donative again by the 1 Edw. VI., they are now nominally elective under the 25 Hen. VIII. In Ireland they are donative by letters patent under the statute of 2 Eliz. This statute must be repealed, as well as all the Acts of Eliz. and Hen. VIII. declaring the supremacy of the Crown in Ecclesiastical matters so far as they relate to Ireland.

Secondly. It would be necessary to change the style or title of the Sovereigns of England. That style is now fixed by statute 35 Hen. VIII. c. 3; by this statute the style of the Sovereign is "Defender of the Faith, and of the Church of England and also of Ireland, in earth the Supreme Head[1]," which latter words are in the abbreviated style of the Sovereign expressed by the words "and so forth." This Act must also be altered.

Thirdly. The whole law of marriage should be changed. At present, with some exceptions, a marriage must be celebrated by a priest in Holy Orders; were the Church disestablished the law would know

[1] Queen Elizabeth, it is true, had a scruple about being styled "Supreme Head," and only styled herself "Supreme Governor;" but the style of the Sovereign never was changed.

nothing of a priest in Holy Orders, the Clergy would be, in the eye of the law, merely the ministers of one of the religious bodies in the country. It would be necessary, therefore, to make marriage a mere civil contract, to which the parties might superadd any ceremony they pleased.

Fourthly. The State could exercise no control or power over public worship. It would no longer be compulsory to use the Book of Common Prayer; the Act of Uniformity should be repealed; no days of public Thanksgiving or Humiliation could be enjoined by the State. Blasphemy would probably still be a *crime*, but to deprave or revile the Christian religion would not; to burn the Bible or Book of Common Prayer in the public highways would be no greater offence than to burn the Koran.

Fifthly. The Bishops should be deprived of their seats in the House of Lords; the number of Irish Peers in the House would be diminished; Ireland would not have her proper proportion of members in that House, so that justice would require that the number of representative Peers should be increased.

Sixthly. It would be necessary to abolish the whole Ecclesiastical law of the country. A parish would be a thing unknown to the law, it would be a mere voluntary arrangement made for convenience by a voluntary association. A parish being unknown, a parishioner could claim no rights except by contract or agreement. The churches and churchyards, now public property, in which every parishioner, whether he conforms to the Church or no, has certain rights, would henceforth become private property, in which no person could have any rights except by contract. It is needless to prosecute the inquiry further; such are a few of the changes which would be the necessary result of disestablishment. Disestablishment is almost exclusively a question of State policy. It is a question for Queen Victoria, whether she is prepared to part with a prerogative her predecessors have enjoyed since the reign of Henry II., and hand down a tarnished Crown to her children. It is, however, only a corollary to the other question of disendowment, in which the Church is vitally interested. In the proposal to disestablish the Church, there is no question of justice or injustice; but the proposal to disendow the Church, as it is mildly called, is, when the origin of her property is considered, one of unparalleled injustice. On this subject the greatest ignorance prevails, and the amount of misrepresentation and falsehood which is circulated throughout the country, quite marvellous. It cannot be too strongly or too frequently asserted, that no dissenter from the Church, be he Protestant or Roman Catholic, contributes one farthing to her maintenance, nor is she in possession of any State provision. The delusion, for it is nothing short of delusion, which prevails on this subject, entirely arises from the erroneous impression that Roman Catholics and dissenters in Ireland are taxed to support the Church.

The property of the Church consists of rent-charge in lieu of tithes, glebe lands and houses, and churches. The latter, Mr. Gladstone is graciously pleased to leave to the Church, if her members are able to sustain them. Tithes are an exclusively Ecclesiastical property. No State ever yet possessed tithes as a species of property or revenue; they originated in the free-will offerings of the faithful ; they were a voluntary gift to the Church, founded upon the Divine ordinance among the Jews, which the Church taught to be equally obligatory upon Christians. The Church claimed them as of Divine right, and Christian nations acknowledged the claim, and enacted laws, not for the purpose of conferring the tithe upon the Church, but to facilitate or enforce the payment of them. Thus the preamble of the statute for payment of tithes recites "that many persons, having no respect to their duties to Almighty God, but against right and conscience, have attempted to substract their tithes due unto God and Holy Church." In process of time they became a distinct species of property, as distinct as the land from the produce of which they were paid, and were and are now held and enjoyed by laymen as well as by Ecclesiastics. Tithes were not paid in the Ancient Irish Church ; they were unknown until the invasion of Ireland by Henry II., and were introduced by the English Ecclesiastics who accompanied him to Ireland to bring the Church of that country into conformity with the Church of England. One of the decrees of the celebrated Council of Cashel, convened by Henry II. in the year 1172, was "that the faithful do pay tithe of animals, corn, and other produce."

This was not a gift or grant by the State to the Church, but it was the assertion of a right by the Church, which it believed to be of Divine origin and sanction, and which the State lent its co-active jurisdiction to enforce. The appropriation of tithes to the maintenance of religious houses was the origin of their coming into the possession of laymen. In Ireland the number of monasteries was very great, as was also the number of parishes, the tithes of which were appropriated to their support. At the suppression of the religious houses—a work commenced by Roman Catholics before the Reformation—some of these tithes were restored to the parishes from whence they were derived, while others were granted to laymen, and much of this species of property became, in consequence of the treason, or alleged treason, of the owners of it, forfeited to the Crown, and a portion of these impropriate tithes so forfeited was by the Crown regranted to the parsons having cure of souls in the parishes from which they were derived, while other portions were granted to laymen. The possession by the Church of tithes, or their substitute tithe rent-charge, cannot be said to be a State provision. It never originated with, nor was conferred by the State, and that portion which was regranted to the Church by the Crown was no gift of the State, inasmuch as such tithes were the private property of the Crown, and could have been retained by the Crown for its own private use.

It is not easy to ascertain the exact condition of the Irish Church as to its property at the time of the English invasion in the reign of Henry II., or even immediately before the Reformation, but whatever its amount or nature, she owed it not to the State, but to the piety and devotion of her own people. During the period that elapsed between the invasion of Henry II. and the Reformation, the civil condition of the country was as bad as it could be,—wasted by continual petty strife among the native chiefs, and by the struggle between the native Irish and the English invaders for the possession of their land. It is not likely that in

these troublous times very much respect was paid to
the property of the Church. We do, however, know
something of the condition of Church property in
Ireland at a later period.

Sir John Davies, Attorney-General for Ireland in
the reign of James I., in a letter to the Earl of
Salisbury, gives an account of a visitation made by
the Lord Deputy, accompanied by the Lord Chan-
cellor, the Lord Chief Justice, Sir Oliver Lambert,
Sir Garret Moore, and himself, in July, 1607, of
the counties of Monaghan, Fermanagh, and Cavan,
during which, in exercise of a commission sent out
of England for the purpose, an inquisition was made
into the state of the Church in those counties. From
which it appeared that in Monaghan " the churches
for the most part were utterly waste : the King was
patron of all of them ; the incumbents were popish
priests instituted by Bishops authorized from Rome,
yet many of them, like other old priests of Queen
Mary's time, in England ready to yield to conformity." Action upon this was reserved " until
the Bishop of Derry, Raphoe, and Clogher, which
three dioceses comprehend the greater part of Ulster
(albeit they be now united for one man's benefit),
should arrive out of England, whose absence, being
two years since he was elected by his Majesty, hath
been the chief cause that no course hath been hitherto
taken to redeem this poor people to Christianity, and
therefore *majus peccatum habet*[2]." In Fermanagh, he

---

[2] This Bishop was George Montgomery, who also held the
deanery of Norwich in England. In 1610 he resigned the Sees
of Derry and Raphoe, and took the administration of Meath,
retaining still the deanery of Norwich. This proves the small
value of the sees of Derry and Raphoe at that time.

writes, " the Church lands were either monastery
land, Corbe ³ land, or Herenach ⁴ land, for it did not
appear the Bishop had any land in demesne, neither did we find the parsons and vicars had any
glebe lands at all in this county. As to monastery
land we found no other than what belonged to the
Abbey of Lisgole, not exceeding two Ballibetaghs ⁵,
for the most part in the barony of Clanawly.
But the lands belonging to the Corbes and Here-
nachs are of far greater quantity. These men possessed all the glebe lands; albeit the incumbents
may be both parsons and vicars, these livings are
not sufficient to feed an honest man." In Cavan
we found " that the greatest number of the parsonages
were appropriated to two great abbeys lying in the
English Pale;" fourteen to the Abbey of Flower in
Westmeath, granted to the Baron of Delwyn, and
eight to the Abbey of Kells, farmed by Gerard
Flemyng; two or three to the Abbey of Cavan,
in the possession of Sir James Dillon." " The
vicarages were so poor as ten of them being united
would scarce maintain an honest minister: that the

---

³ Corbe was a prior or resident in a Collegiate Church.
⁴ The Herenach was in almost every parish. When a layman
founded a church, he dedicated a good portion of land to some
saint, and gave it to a clerk not in orders and his heirs for ever
upon trust, to keep the church clean and repaired, to keep hospitality, and give alms to the poor. He was called Erenach; he
had *primam tonsuram*, but no other orders; he had a voice in the
Chapter, and paid a rent yearly to the Bishop, also a fine upon
the marriage of each of his daughters, and a subsidy to the Bishop
on his first entrance into his bishopric.
⁵ Ballibetagh means a town able to maintain hospitality; it
was equal to 960 acres. The whole of Monaghan contained
86,000 acres.

churches for the most part were in ruins, and covered only with thatch. That the incumbents, both parsons and vicars, did appear such poor, ragged, ignorant creatures (for we saw many of them in the camp), as we could not deem any of them worthy of the meanest of those livings, albeit many of them are not worth 40s. per annum. This county doth lie within the diocese of Kilmore, whose Bishop, Robert Draper, is parson of Trim⁶, the best parsonage in the whole kingdom—a man of this country's birth—worth well-nigh 400l. a year. He doth now live in those parts where he hath two bishoprics⁷, but there is no Divine Service or Sermon to be· heard within either of his dioceses.'

In 1633, Archbishop Bramhall, then Archdeacon of Meath, was employed in a royal visitation along with Baron Hilton, the Judge of the Prerogative, and writing to Archbishop Laud, August 10, 1633, he says, "that they found the bishoprics in particular wretchedly dilapidated by fee farms and long leases at small rents granted partly by the Popish Bishops, who resolved to carry as much with them as they could, and partly by their Protestant successors, who might fear another turn,· and were, having their example, disposed enough to make use of the same arts. By such means many Bishoprics were made extremely small, some reduced to 100l. a year, some to 50l., as Waterford, Kilfenora; some to five marks⁸, as Kilmacduagh, and particularly

---

⁶ He held Trim *in commendam*, on account of the low state of the revenues of the bishopric.

⁷ The other bishopric was Ardagh. This prelate was appointed by King James, because he knew *the Irish language ! !*

⁸ The mark was 13s. 4d.

Cloyne, the Bishop whereof was called Episcopus quinque Marcarum; Aghadoe was only 1*l*. 1*s*. 8*d*., and Ardfert but 60*l*. Limerick had above five parts in six made away by fee farms or encroached on by undertakers. The like was done in Cashel, Emly, Waterford, Lismore, and Killaloe." After this period the Rebellion of 1641 broke out, which was succeeded by the invasion of Cromwell and his fanatics, who persecuted with all the zeal of religious bigotry the Bishops and Clergy of the Irish Church, as well as the Roman Catholics, and other loyalists of Ireland. The Bishops were driven from their Sees, the Clergy from their Benefices, and the Church lay prostrate for fourteen years, during which no very tender regard was paid to her property. So that at the period of the restoration of Charles II. the condition of the property of the Church was most deplorable.

I shall now very briefly point out some of the sources from which the Church has derived her present property. I regret that the information I can give upon this subject is so meagre; but I trust it will be sufficient to show that the confiscation of Church property in Ireland would be a very gross violation of the rights of property.

In consequence of the Earl of Tyrone's rebellion, there were large counties and tracts of land forfeited to the Crown: in the six counties of Donegal, Tyrone, Derry, Fermanagh, Cavan, and Armagh, as much as 500,000 acres. These counties had been wasted during the rebellion; great numbers of the inhabitants had perished by the sword and famine, and the rest were so reduced in poverty that they could not manure the land,—so that it was likely to remain waste for want of people or riches to cultivate and improve it. These lands were allotted by King James I., under the advice of Sir Arthur Chichester, Lord Deputy, among three classes of people: (1) The old Irish chieftains and inhabitants; (2) The Servitors of the Crown, who were either the great officers of state or the captains and officers who had served in the army; and (3) English and Scotch adventurers. Great indulgence was given to the Irish chiefs, even those who had been implicated in Tyrone's rebellion. Their under-tenants were allowed to be of their own country and *religion*, being exempted from the Oath of Supremacy, which the tenants of the other planters were obliged to take. The British undertakers being allowed to have none but English or Scotch; and the Servitors, though permitted to employ natives, were yet bound to employ none but Protestants. The estate of the bishoprics were in Ulster altogether unprofitable to the Bishops, partly being claimed by the temporal Lords, and partly by the claims of the patentees, who included in their patents the Church lands, not excepting the site of Cathedral Churches and the places of residence of Bishops, Deans, and Canons. Most of the Parochial Churches had been destroyed in the rebellion, or fallen down for want of roofs. The livings were very small; and for years Divine Service had not been used in any parish throughout Ulster, except in some city or principal town. King James ordered all Ecclesiastical lands to be restored to their respective Sees and Churches, that compositions should be made with the patentees for the site of Cathedral Churches and the houses of residence of Bishops and dignities, which were never intended to be granted to them—an equivalent to be allowed to the patentees. He ordered the Bishops to give up all impropriations to the respective Incumbents, recompensing them with grants of his own lands. He caused every portion allotted to undertakers to be made a parish, and a Parochial Church to be erected therein, the Incumbent whereof was (besides the tithes) to have a glebe set out to him of 60, 90, or 120 acres, according to the size of the parish. These orders of the King were but badly observed by the Commissioners, who were too intent on their private interest. Glebes were set out in inconvenient places, sometimes out of the district of the parish to the Church of which they belonged; and the Clergy defrauded if not in the quantity generally in quality of the land assigned to them; and thus King James's pious intentions were, in a great measure, defeated.

On the restoration of King Charles II., he found that a large portion of the country had been forfeited and escheated to the Crown, in consequence of the rebellion of 1641. Whether these forfeitures were just or not it would be idle now to inquire. I am not one of those patriots who love to dwell on the dark pages of my country's history, or think the welfare and happiness of my countrymen are best promoted by reminding them continually of the wrongs, if wrongs they be, perpetrated two centuries ago. At this period of our history property forfeited to the Crown became as much its private property as the property of any of the nobility; and it was quite competent for the Crown to retain the possession of it or to bestow it on whom it pleased. The forfeited estates in Ireland were, however, pledged to recom-

pense those English officers and soldiers who, as
adventurers, volunteered to suppress the rebellion, and
secure the country for the Crown of England ; subject
to this they were the absolute property of the Crown—
its private property.

The Act of Settlement, 14 and 15 Car. II., c. 2,
s. 97, restored to Ecclesiastical persons all property of
which " they were possessed in the year of our Lord
1641, and from which they had been dispossessed
during the fury and violence of the late times." Sect.
98 vested all leases for terms of years of Ecclesiastical lands forfeited to his Majesty in the Ecclesiastical persons entitled to the reversion expectant on
such leases. The effect of these provisions was merely
to restore to the Church that which had been its own,
the Crown declining to take advantage of the forfeiture occasioned by the treason of the Ecclesiastical
tenants. The 99th sect. of the same Act provided,
that out of the *Ecclesiastical lands* which had been
granted or conveyed in fee-farm and had been forfeited
to his Majesty, certain portions should be granted by
way of augmentation to the Archbishops of Dublin and
Cashel, and the Bishops of Kildare, Clonfert, Ferns
and Leighlin, Limerick, Ossory, and Killaloe. And
sect. 101 provided that the same rent should be paid
to his Majesty for said lands as was paid by the adventurers and soldiers for the lands allotted to them. By
the Act of Explanation, 17 & 18 Car. II., sec. 27, it
was provided, that in lieu of the provision contained in
the Act of Settlement for Glebes, the Commissioners
were to set out so many acres of land as might be
sufficient to endow all and every the parochial Churches
with ten acres, except such as have already the like or

a greater quantity of glebe, subject to a rent to his Majesty; and, by the 28th sect., impropriate or appropriate tithes vested in his Majesty were granted to the Incumbents of the parishes from which they did arise.

It seems impossible to contend that the Church by these means is possessed of a State endowment, or that it owes its property to the State more than some of the first families in Ireland who hold their estates under the selfsame title. · These provisions amount to no more than a regrant to the Church of property of which she had been despoiled in the troublous times, or grants to her by the·King of his own property out of his Royal Bounty. The nation had nothing to say to it. This may be illustrated by the 122 sect. of the Act of Explanation (17 & 18 Car. II.), by which " all messuages, manors, lands, &c., whereof Sir John Fitzgerald died seised in the year 1640, which were then belonging to the Bishop of Cloyne and his successors, and were by the will of the said Sir John Fitzgerald, dated 18th Sept. 1640, devised to King Car. I., were granted to the Bishop of Cloyne and his successors, except the rectories and impropriate tithes therein bequeathed to his said Majesty, which rectories and impropriate tithes were settled upon the Incumbents and their successors having cure of souls in the several parishes from which they arose, and the patronage of the said Churches was vested in his Majesty, his heirs and successors." This surely is no State provision. The property was devised to King Charles I., and inherited from him by King Charles II., who of his own bounty granted it to the Church; and so it was as to the forfeited lands. By the forfeiture they became

the private property of the Crown, and were granted
to the Church by it.

The first-fruits and twentieth part of all Ecclesiastical benefices were payable to the Crown, and formed
part of its income.   In the year 1711 Queen Anne re-
mitted to the Clergy the twentieth parts, and granted
a patent vesting the first-fruits in trustees, to be applied
for ever towards purchasing glebes, building houses, and
buying impropriations for the use of the Clergy.   In
1726 the Bishops, finding that the first-fruits were
very inadequate for the purpose intended, considerably
augmented them by private subscriptions, and the Clergy
also generously contributed.   And up to the year 1780
there had been sixteen glebes purchased at the cost of
3543*l*. 2*s*. 7*d*., and tithes for fourteen Incumbents, for
5855*l*. 13*s*. 6*d*., and assistance given for the building
of forty-five glebe houses, by gifts of 4080*l*.   It is
true that very large sums were annually voted by Parliament in augmentation of this fund from the time of
the union up to the year 1823, but during that period
a sum of 102,598*l*. 4*s*. 2*d*. was repaid to the trustees
by the Clergy out of their incomes, being advances
made to them to assist in building glebe houses.   The
parliamentary grant during this period was very large,
amounting in the whole to about 507,320*l*.; out of this
sum 56,394*l*. was expended in purchasing glebes and a
considerable sum was spent in building Churches.   The
property thus acquired, so far as regards the first-fruits
and their augmentation by private subscriptions, was
clearly not derived from the State, but from the private bounty of the Queen, and the Bishops and Clergy.
The only portion of it that can be said to have been
derived from the State, is that which is the produce of

the parliamentary grants. These grants have ceased to be made since the year 1823. They were granted for a purpose then deemed desirable ; namely, to provide residences for the Clergy, and build Churches throughout the country—their purpose has been fulfilled ; and no case can be made for undoing what was then done, for pulling down the Churches and glebe houses, which have been erected by the assistance of these grants.

The Church has also acquired much property from the benevolence and piety of her own people since the Reformation.

Archbishop BRAMHALL purchased abundance of impropriations, either with his own money, or by large remittances from England (Archbishop Laud gave 40,000*l.* for this purpose out of his own purse), by money given by his Majesty for pious uses, by borrowing large sums, and securing them out of the issues of the impropriations he bought, by voluntary contributions, and by a share of the goods of persons dying intestate. By these and other means he regained to the Church 30,000*l.* a year.

In 1567 the See of Armagh was so poor that ADAM LOFTUS accepted the Archbishopric of Dublin ; and his successor, Thomas Lancaster, had a licence from Queen Elizabeth to hold, *in commendam*, the treasurership of Salisbury, the rectory of Southhill, in the diocese of Exeter, the rectory of Sherfield, in the diocese of Winchester, the archdeaconry of Kells, together with the rectory of Nobber, and the prebend of Stagonil, in the Cathedral of St. Patrick's, Dublin, on account of the poverty of the See.

Archbishop HENRY USSHER obtained, in 1611, a

grant to him and his successors, Archbishops of Armagh, of the manor of Donoghmore and eight town lands in Iveagh, in the county of Down, to be holden of the Crown in frankalmoigne, and also a grant of of three town lands in Iveagh, to Patrick O'Connor O'Kearney and his heirs, to be holden of the Archbishop and his successors, as of his manor of Donoghmore, by fealty and suit of court, and the yearly rent of 6l.

Archbishop HAMPTON (1613—1624) built from the foundation a handsome palace at Drogheda for himself and his successors, at a cost of 2064l., and repaired the Cathedral of St. Patrick at Armagh, which had been ruined by Shane O'Neill, and the steeple demolished. He also cast the great bell, and repaired an old Episcopal house at Armagh, to which he added new buildings, and annexed 300 acres of land near the town of Armagh for mensal lands to the See.

Archbishop BRAMHALL, by his will, dated Jan. 5, 1662, left 500l. towards the repair of the Cathedral of Armagh and of St. Peter's at Drogheda, over and above such sums as he should bestow on them in his lifetime. He repaired the Episcopal house at Drogheda, which he found in ruins.

Archbishop MARGETSON (1663—1678) rebuilt the Cathedral of Armagh, which had been burnt by O'Neill, by his own money, and contributions collected throughout Ireland, and also repaired and adorned his Episcopal palace, and contributed largely to the repair of the two Cathedrals in Dublin.

Archbishop NARCISSUS MARSH left his estate of Stormanstown in Meath to the Vicars Choral of Armagh.

Archbishop MICHAEL BOYLE (1678—1702) built in the town of Blessington, near Dublin, a magnificent country house, an elegant chapel, a parish Church and steeple, which he furnished with a peal of six bells : his monument is still in the Church.

Archbishop THOMAS LYNDSAY (1713—1724) purchased the organ and a ring of six bells for the Cathedral of Armagh, and bequeathed 1000*l.* to be laid out in the purchase of 50*l.* a year for the economy of Armagh. During his life he laid out 4000*l.* in the purchase of lands which he annexed to the ancient estate belonging to the choir. His munificence to the Church in his lifetime and by will amounted to about 7000*l.*

Primate BOULTER left a very large sum of money for the purchase of glebes for the Clergy, and the augmentation and improvement of small livings. This sum is at present invested in 36,232*l.* 7*s.* 3*d.*, 3 per cent. Stock; 38,700*l.*, Bank of Ireland Stock; and 14,750*l.*, 3 per cent. Consols.

Primate ROBINSON left 1000*l.* for the same purpose. These bequests of Primates Boulter and Robinson are at present administered by the Ecclesiastical Commissioners of Ireland, and yield an annual income of about 4700*l.*

Primate ROBINSON also built the palace at Armagh, and four Churches, a school, a public library, to which he gave a large collection of books, also a market-house and shambles.

Lord JOHN GEORGE BERESFORD, Archbishop (1822 —1862), spent nearly 30,000*l.* in restoring the Cathedral of Armagh.

In the diocese of Meath : —

GEORGE MONTGOMERY, Bishop (1610—1620), built a palace at Ardbraccan, and repaired the Church.

JOHN EVANS, Bishop (1715—1723), bequeathed 1000*l*. to build the Episcopal house at Ardbraccan, and his personal estate to the Archbishop of Armagh and Bishop of Meath, to purchase glebe and impropriate tithes for the endowment of the several Churches in the diocese of Meath, in the sole donation of the Bishop of that See. Ardbraccan House was afterwards built by Bishop Price (1733), from the design of this Bishop.

HENRY MAULE, Bishop, by his will, dated October 5, 1757, bequeathed 100*l*. to the Bishop of Cloyne, for the purchase of glebe and tithes for one poor living in that diocese.

In the diocese of Clogher :—

RICHARD TENNISON, Bishop (1690—1697), repaired and beautified the palace, and built out-offices, and increased its revenues at least a third part.

JOHN STERNE, Bishop (1717), left 80*l*. a year for a catechist to be chosen by the Clergy of the city of Dublin every third year; to building a spire on the top of St. Patrick's steeple, 100*l*. ; to the trustees of first-fruits, 2000*l*., to be laid out in the purchase of glebes or impropriate tithes ; 1500*l*. or 2000*l*., as his executors should think proper, towards finishing the Cathedral of Clogher, with other charitable bequests.

In the diocese of Dromore :—

King JAMES I., by letters patent, granted to William Worsey, of Hotham, in Northamptonshire, certain lands to hold to him and his heirs, of the Bishop of Dromore and his successors, in free and common soccage, as of his manor of Dromore, at the rent of 40*l*., on condition he should build a stone-house, in or near Dromore, and lay out a curtilage of one acre as a mansion-house for the Bishop and his successors, and the said Worsey covenanted to grant to every Incumbent of Garvagh, Magherawly, and Dromore, in Iveagh, sixty acres adjoining each of the said churches and chapels, as glebe lands for the same.

THEOPHILUS BUCKWORTH, Bishop (1613), expended 500*l*. in additional buildings to the See house.

JEREMY TAYLOR (1661), administrator of the diocese, rebuilt the Church of Dromore at his own expense.

In the diocese of Raphoe :—

JOHN POOLEY, Bishop (1702), left 200*l*. to improve the Cathedral.

NICHOLAS FORSTER, Bishop (1716), erected chapels-of-ease in large parishes, founded a school in the town of Raphoe, endowed a house in Raphoe, with lands of the value of 75*l*. a year, for the widows of four clergymen. In 1737 he laid out 700*l*. in re-building the diocesan school-house. He built a steeple on the Cathedral. He bequeathed the money due by his successors to him for improvements (427*l*.), together with 600*l*. to the Bishop and Archdeacon of Raphoe, to be paid to the Bishop of Raphoe, to lay out 12*l*. a year in repairing parish Churches, and 6*l*. a year for repairing the Cathedral.

In the diocese of Down and Connor :—

Bishop HUTCHINSON, with the aid of contributions from the neighbouring gentry and Clergy, built a new Church in the year 1723 in the island of Raghery, off the coast of Antrim, and by means of the first-fruits bought the great tithes of the island for the endowment of the minister.

In the diocese of Derry :—

EZEKIEL HOPKINS, Bishop (1681,) was at great expense in beautifying and adorning his Cathedral, in furnishing it with an organ and massive plate. He spent 1000l. in buildings and other improvements in Derry and Raphoe.

BERNARD, WILLIAM, Bishop (1747), built a chapel-of-ease, adjacent to the city walls and the Episcopal palace.

LORD BRISTOL, Bishop (1768), built the glebe house and chapel-of-ease in Tamlaght O'Crilly, and almost rebuilt the Bishop's palace.

KNOX, WILLIAM, Bishop (1808), expended 3000l. on the Cathedral, and built the free Church at Derry.

In the diocese of Dublin :—

NARCISSUS MARSH (1694 — 1702) endowed an almshouse in Drogheda for the reception of twelve widows of decayed clergymen, to each of whom he allotted a lodging and 20l. a year. He gave 40l. a year to the Dean and Chapter of Armagh, he repaired several Churches at his own expense, bought in several impropriations and restored them to the Church.

WILLIAM KING (1702), when Bishop of Derry, purchased some advowsons which he added to the See, and largely contributed to building five new Churches, and repairing all in his diocese. He purchased from Lord Ross a large quantity of impropriate tithes in Kildare for 2800l. for augmenting cures in his diocese; also lands near Dublin, and annexed them to his See ; and also 49l. a year, part of the estate of Sir John

Eccles, at 1050*l.*, and settled it for the support of a lecturer in St. George's Church, Dublin. He spent 3000*l.* on the See house of St. Sepulchre, and built a court-house for the manor ; he recovered the lands of Seaton, and had them settled on the See by Act of Parliament. He purchased the lay rectories of Crevagh in the county of Dublin, Ballytemple and New Castle in the county of Wicklow, and collated Incumbents thereto. He purchased 40*l.* a year impropriate tithes from Mr. Wentworth. He devised 400*l.* to the Archbishop of Tuam and Bishop of Clogher, to purchase glebes for one or more Churches in the diocese of Dublin and in 1726, he gave 300*l.* to the Board of First-Fruits for purchasing glebes and impropriate tithes for the increase of small livings.

In the diocese of Ossory :—

JOHN WHEELER, Bishop (1613), at great expense recovered the See lands, which Bishop Thonery (in the time of Queen Mary) had alienated. Had a grant by patent, 23rd December, 1619, of 1000 acres arable land, wood, and pasture, and 139 acres bog in the plantation and territory of Ely O'Carroll ; to hold the arable land, wood, and pasture in frankalmoigne, and the bog in free and common soccage of the Castle of Dublin at the yearly rent of 5*s.* 9*d.*, with the creation of these premises into a manor.

GRIFFITH WILLIAMS, Bishop, laid out 1400*l.* in the repairs of the Cathedral of St. Cunice. The ring of bells had been carried away in the rebellion of 1641. He gave a large bell which cost 144*l.*, repaired the chancel at a cost of 300*l.*, and laid out 40*l.* on the belfry.

JOHN PARRY, Bishop (1672), laid out 400*l.* in re-

c 2

pairing the Episcopal house. In 1675 he gave a ring of six bells to the Cathedral, which cost 246*l*. 13*s*. 10*d*. He made a present of three bells to three Churches, viz. Gowran, Calan, and Thomastown. He passed patents for the augmentation lands granted under the Act of Settlement, and for many impropriations to the use of the Clergy of his diocese; for thirteen rectories. He gave by will 200*l*. to Christ Church, Dublin, to buy a pair of large silver candlesticks gilt, and other utensils for the use of the altar, and 100*l*. to buy plate for the Cathedral of Kilkenny.

THOMAS OTWAY, Bishop (1679), founded the library at the Cathedral of St. Canice; he bequeathed 60*l*. to be distributed equally to the repairs of the Churches of Gowran, Castlecomer, and Durrow; he bought plate for the Cathedral, which had belonged to Christ Church, Dublin, for 116*l*. 13*s*. 4*d*.; he beautified the Cathedral, and erected an organ. He recovered many of the augmentation lands, which had been given to his See.

CHARLES ESTE, Bishop (1735), laid out 1935*l*. in improving the See house.

MICHAEL COX, Bishop (1743), laid out 300*l*. on the house; he refused a fine of 700*l*. for land, held by Lord Shelburne, which he converted into a demesne at the cost of 500*l*.

The diocese of Ferns:—

The See lands had been alienated by Bishop Devereux and by Bishop Hugh Allen, some of which were recovered at great expense by Bishop RAM. This Bishop found the revenues of his See reduced from 400*l*. or 500*l*. a year to 66*l*. 6*s*. 8*d*. He recovered the manor of Fethard, and the town-land of Hevington by law. He built the Episcopal house at Old Leighlin, and left a library for the use of the Clergy.

BARTHOLOMEW VIGERS, Bishop (1690), purchased from Joseph Dean, Esq., chief Baron of the Exchequer, a fee-farm in the manor of Old Leighlin for 548*l.*, which he devised by will to his successors. He also left 300*l.* to be laid out by the advice of the Archbishop of Dublin in augmenting the See of Leighlin.

WALTER COPE, Bishop, built the See house at Ferns.

The diocese of Cashel :—

EDMUND BUTLER, Bishop (1527), recovered at great expense the See lands from John Fitz-Theobald Burke.

The diocese of Waterford :—

HUGH GORE, Bishop (1690), laid out considerable sums in beautifying the Cathedral of Waterford. By will he gave 200*l.* to provide a ring of bells for the Church of Lismore, and beautifying the choir ; 100*l.* towards buying a ring of bells for the Church of Clonmel. The residue of his real and personal estate, after some other charitable bequests, he left for building and repairing old ruinated Churches in Waterford and Lismore. This property consists of 3381*l.* 3*s.* 9*d.*, 3 per cent. stock, and 374*l.* 15*s.* 10*d.* per annum tithe rent-charge from the parish of Cahir, in the diocese of Lismore, and is at present administered by the Ecclesiastical Commissioners for Ireland.

Bishop CHENEVIX, by will, dated 13th August, 1777, bequeathed to the diocese of Waterford, 1600*l.*, the interest to be given to the widows of clergymen of that diocese, and 1000*l.* to the diocese of Lismore, to be expended for the benefit of that diocese at the discretion of the Bishop of the diocese for the time being.

In the diocese of Cloyne, Cork, and Ross :—

EDWARD SYNGE, Bishop (1663), by will devised two plough-lands of Ballycroneen, which he had purchased from John Fitz-Thomas Gerald, to the Bishop of Cloyne and his successors.

EDWARD WETENHALL, Bishop (1678), repaired the ruinous Episcopal houses of Cork and Kilmore, and rebuilt the Cathedral Church of Ardagh.

PETER BROWN, Bishop (1609), expended 2000l. on a country-house at Ballynaspeck, or Bishopstown, near Cork, and left it to his successors, as also his improvements at Bishopscourt, in Cork, of great value.

CHARLES CROW, Bishop (1702), at his own expense, recovered to the see of Cloyne the manor of Donnoghmore, containing 8000 acres of land, plantation measure.

In the diocese of Killaloe :—

SIR THOMAS VESEY settled the rectorial tithes of Abbeyleix, part of his private estate, on the vicar; and after he was translated to Ossory, he repaired and improved his Palace at Kilkenny.

In the diocese of Tuam :—

JOHN VESEY, Bishop (1678), by will directed 400l. to be laid out in the purchase of lands or tithes for the Economy of Tuam, to be conveyed to the Dean and Chapter of Tuam, and gave to the Dean and Chapter the impropriate tithes of the lands of Dubdowlagh and Ballyglass in the county of Galway.

In the diocese of Elphin :—

EDWARD KING, Bishop (1611), repaired the Cathedral at his own expense. He built a castle, and some offices adjoining to it at Elphin, for himself and his successors, and endowed it with lands which he had purchased. His bishopric, which he found reduced to 200 marks, he left worth 1500*l.* a year.

JOHN HUDSON, Bishop (1667), devised 566*l.* to erect a new house where the old castle stood, for the Bishop of Elphin and his successors.

In the diocese of Killala :—

THOMAS OTWAY, Bishop (1670), rebuilt the cathedral of Killala from the foundation, as also a parish Church in his diocese.

Such are a few of the gifts to the Church by her own Bishops only, which a very imperfect search has enabled me to trace, and I have no doubt but that a diligent search among the records of the country, and of the different dioceses, would not only find many more, but would also prove that the laity and inferior Clergy have also largely contributed to those endowments which the Church is now possessed of, and of which it is said she must now be despoiled in order to do *justice* to the Roman Catholics of Ireland ! !

Such being the nature of the Church's title, would it not be an act of the grossest injustice to take from her property so acquired ? What right has the State to take possession of, or divert these endowments to other purposes ?

I am free to admit that when a man grants his property to the endowment of a public institution, or for a public object, he dedicates it to the public, and the nation has a perfect right to mould that institution, so as may be most beneficial, and even should it become injurious to society, to abolish it, and apply the property so granted to other public purposes; but, however, only to such as are as cognate as possible to those for which the donor intended it. But so long as the institution continues, so long as it is suffered by the State to exist, it is contrary to every principle of right and justice, to that natural justice, which even heathen lawyers recognized, that its property should be alienated, and applied to purposes for which it was never intended by the donors. To disendow the Irish Church, as is proposed by Mr. Gladstone, to alienate its property and apply it to other, perhaps secular purposes, would be an act of injustice unparalleled in the history of any civilized nation; it would be so monstrous a wrong, such an outrage on every principle of right and equity, that I cannot believe it possible that a British House of Commons, when really informed on the subject, will ever consent to it. It may possibly be said, that a similar wrong was perpetrated at the Reformation; but it is not so: no portion of the property of the Church was confiscated or alienated at the Reformation; the property of the religious houses was confiscated, and a portion of this property was granted to the Church; but then the institutions themselves were condemned. I am far from saying that no wrong was done at this time; nay, much was done which we have every reason to regret and deplore. But, be it remembered, that the whole of this evil is not attributable to the Reformation; the suppression of the religious houses commenced *before* the Reformation, and they were even then condemned as encouraging indolence and slothful living,—justly or unjustly, however, the institutions themselves were condemned.

They were declared hurtful to society, and therefore society had a right to apply their revenues to other purposes. But even in the suppression of the monasteries, whatever injustice or wrong was perpetrated, the forms of law and right were observed; they were all formally surrendered to the Crown; no doubt those surrenders can hardly be said to have been voluntary; nevertheless, the perpetrators of this wrong, if wrong it was, felt themselves bound to observe the forms at least of right. The Reformation affords no precedent for such a wrong as is now contemplated by Mr. Gladstone's scheme. What offence has the Church of Ireland committed to justify this confiscation of her property? What has she done to call for the enactment of this penal law? Are her Clergy preachers of sedition or the abettors of crime? Are her people disloyal or disaffected? On the contrary; it is admitted, that they are the most loyal, the most civilized, the most industrious, and the most peaceable portion of the community. Even the leader of this assault upon her, the most active promoter of this penal code, admits that she brings to the people of this country that truth which is of all possessions the most precious to the souls of men [9]. Why, then, is she to be plundered and her property confiscated? It is said she has failed to effect the object for which she was founded—that she is a missionary Church, and her mission has failed. They who urge this objection to her, speak as if the Irish Church was founded, 300 years ago, for the purpose of converting the Roman Catholics of Ireland, nay, some of those who under-

[9] See "A Chapter of Autobiography," by Right Hon. W. E. Gladstone, M.P.

took her defence in the late Parliament argued on the same assumption.

The Church of Ireland, however, the church of St. Patrick and St. Columba, boasts of an earlier origin. Nor is she a missionary Church in any other sense than the whole Christian Church is missionary. Her mission is to turn the hearts of the disobedient to the wisdom of the just. I should much regret that the Clergy of the Irish Church should ever believe it to be their chief and paramount duty to endeavour to convert the Roman Catholic population of this country to Protestantism. No doubt it is their duty, in season, to teach the truth, and they would rejoice were they able to bring any of the Roman Catholics to abandon the doctrinal errors, and the superstitious, and worse than superstitious, practices of the Church of Rome. But it never can be their duty to keep continually alive the baneful spirit of religious controversy. The Irish Clergy, without entering upon controversy at all, or endeavouring to unsettle the faith of their Roman Catholic parishioners, may do much to encourage amongst them those great Christian virtues, acknowledged by all, and which, after all, are the fruit by which the tree is to be tried. The great offence charged against the Irish Church is, that she has not gained over the great bulk of the people. But she has had much to contend against; not the least of her obstacles has been the inveterate hatred of England, which has so long existed in the breast of the Irish peasant, a hatred, which has not its origin in the difference of religious belief. It originated when England was Roman Catholic. The famous statute of Kilkenny was passed by the English Roman Catholic Colonists.

The native Irish were treated as enemies, they were outlawed, and would not be admitted to the protection or benefit of English law, however much they might desire it. The Reformation originating in England was of itself enough to arouse the hostility of the Irish; the language of the people also, as in Wales, formed a serious barrier to its progress; the Statute of 2 Eliz. c. 2 (the Act of Uniformity) provided that if a priest was ignorant of the English language he might perform the service in Latin, and although the statute prescribed that this Latin Service should be according to the Book of Common Prayer, yet it is well known that the Latin edition of the Prayer Book of Elizabeth never was circulated or in use in Ireland, and consequently the service which was used in those parts of Ireland, where the Clergy were ignorant of English, must have been the old Roman Service. The Reformation in the reign of Henry VIII. was one more in Ecclesiastical polity, that in doctrine, the Irish Act, 28 Hen. VIII., c. 13, contains a clause which is not in the corresponding English Act, viz. "that the Act nor any thing therein should be in any wise prejudicial, hurtful, or derogatory to the ceremonies, uses, and other laudable and politic ordinances for a true tranquillity, discipline, concord, devotion, unity, and the decent order *heretofore* in the Church of Ireland, used, instituted, taken and accepted;" thus maintaining the old ceremonies and services of the Roman Liturgy. Besides, even in those parts of the country where the English Service was used, it must have been as unintelligible to the mass of the people as the old service. The civil condition of the country, rent by civil war, created an effectual barrier to the spread of either civilization or religion.

It was not until the reign of James I. that English law
obtained any firm footing in the country, or that there
was any cessation from internal discord. After thirty
years of peace, and some progress made in establishing
order and religion, the Church was overthrown by the
Cromwellians, and the barbarous cruelties practised
by these fanatics increased the hostility of the people
both to England and the English Reformation.

But according to Mr. Gladstone the great proof
that the Irish Church is powerless to effect what he
supposes to be her mission is that for the last thirty
years, since the termination of what is known in
Ireland as the tithe war, the Church has enjoyed
advantages such as can hardly be expected to recur,
ample endowments, perfect security, freedom from
controversy (which controversy has, however, improved the Church of England), and *the knowledge
of the Irish language has been extensively attained by
the Clergy!* While in the Church of Rome her
people have been borne down by famine and thinned
by emigration, and yet at the census of 1861 only
"the faintest impression has been made upon the
relative numbers of the two bodies [1]." The Protestant
poor, however, suffered just as much in the famine of
1846 as the Roman Catholic, and the small Protestant
farmers have emigrated in large numbers; besides this,
the poorer classes in every state increase more rapidly,
both relatively and actually, than the classes above
them in social position, so that little reliance can be
placed on this, even if it were any, test of the efficiency
of a Church. But if the efficiency of a Church is to be
thus tested, what are we to say of the Church of

[1] "A Chapter of Autobiography," p. 34.

England ? At the Reformation she gained the whole
population, she had no prejudices to contend against,
and the Bible and Book of Common Prayer being in
the language of the people, they not only could under-
stand the services, but they could appreciate the benefits of the change. Yet she has lost more than a third
of the population, who have fallen off to Romanism and
Protestant dissent. And during the last thirty years,
with ample endowments, in perfect peace, her Episco-
pacy increased, we have witnessed a secession from her
communion of an amount of talent, piety, and wealth unparalleled in her history. In truth, however, the efficiency of a Church is not to be tested by the number of
her converts, but by the lives and character of her own
people ; and brought to this test I deny that the Irish
Church has failed. On the contrary, there is to be
found among her people a great increase in religion
and piety, a great abstinence from vices that were
fashionable fifty years ago, an increased devotion in
her public services, a greater number of Churches
and faithful, painstaking pastors. There is scarcely a
parish in the country in which the public worship of
God is not maintained according to the forms of the
Reformed Church. Civilization and prosperity have
followed in her train ; nay, the Church of Rome herself has greatly benefited by her presence. Why have
we not in Ireland those superstitious practices which
disgrace the public worship of the Roman Church in
other countries? Why have we not winking Madonnas,
liquefaction of the blood of deceased martyrs, or a
post-office to the Virgin Mary ? Are not the Irish
superstitious enough to believe in such things ? The
truth is, such practices could not stand the light, and

dare not be attempted in the presence of the Reformed Church.

Another objection urged against the Irish Church is that she is a badge of conquest, and a remnant of an odious ascendancy. What conquest? The conquest of Ireland by England! It was Pope Urban II. that urged the English to the conquest, and granted the country to Henry II. The Reformation is no doubt English, but is it the only thing English in the country, and are there not more real badges of conquest than it? Is it not a badge of conquest that Ireland should be ruled by an English Queen—that her nobility should consist chiefly of Englishmen— that her great landed proprietors should be English absentees—that her legislature should sit in England —are not these more, much more substantial badges of slavery and conquest than the Reformed Church? And as to ascendancy—where is it? It consists in this, and this only, that it is the undoubted right of the Crown to create Bishoprics in Ireland, and to appoint Bishops to them, and therefore the Pope cannot do so. It is the ascendancy of the Crown, in her own kingdom over a foreign Potentate—a Potentate, too, who would not allow the Queen of England to build even one Church within his own capital. Yet the Roman Catholic bishops are respected and treated with all the deference due to their sacred office; the clergy, if they are not called rectors of parishes, are called by a much higher designation, parish priests. It is true as a class they do not occupy the same social position as the Clergy of the Reformed Church; but that is because as a body they are taken from a lower grade in society. This, however, will not be remedied by disendowing the Church. The only consequences of such a measure will be to substitute for educated gentlemen, of whom at present the Clergy of the Established Church are composed, an ignorant, bigoted, and inferior class of Clergy.

Why, then, are the Bishops and Clergy of the Irish Church to be deprived of their property? Where is the justice to Roman Catholics in spoliating the Church of that property, which she has received from the piety of her own members? Why is this wrong to be inflicted on the Reformed Church, this wanton injustice which is to confer no benefit on any one in the whole country? The promoters of the spoliation themselves have not even yet discovered to what purposes this property is to be diverted. It would seem that any purpose whatever would be in their judgments better than that for which it was originally designed, and to which it has hitherto been applied, viz. the public worship of Almighty God. Does even the new fangled doctrine of religious equality, which seems to have as much sense in it as the Communist theory of social equality, call for or demand this act of spoliation? If the State is, according to this novel theory, to separate herself from the Church, why should she carry off with her property, which does not and never did belong to her. Disestablish the Church, if it must be so. Let the State ignore all religious bodies impartially; but why should she, merely to gratify the bigotry or pride of those who dissent from the Church, perpetrate a wrong and injustice unparalleled in the history of civilized Europe? Adopt the precedent afforded by the Church of Canada, if it must be so. Make the Church perfectly free from

State control and State patronage. The machinery
is at hand. Empower the Primate to convene Convocation, and enable Convocation, when convened, to
regulate all the affairs of the Church, to make canons
and constitutions for the decision of all questions of
doctrine and discipline, for the election and conse-
cration of Bishops, for the creation or union of sees
and parishes, and for the ordering of Divine Service
without the control of the Parliament, the Crown, or the
civil courts; incorporate, if necessary, the Upper House
of Convocation with power to hold property; recog-
nize its judicial functions as regards the Clergy; give
Convocation or diocesan synods power to regulate the
property of the Church, the distribution and administration of its revenues. In all this, whatever other
wrong there may be, there will, at all events, be no
injustice, no spoliation. I do not say it is to be
desired; but if it be forced upon the Church, if the
State is no longer to have any religion, such a measure will, at all events, not be fraught with injustice.

It is true, that in Canada the Clergy reserves have
been secularized; but there is no analogy between the
circumstances of Canada and of Ireland.

Upon the conquest of Canada, the Roman Catholic
clergy were permitted to retain all dues and tithes
payable by those of their own communion.

A large number of persons, chiefly members of
the Church of England, emigrated from America into
Canada; to supply their spiritual wants missionary
Clergy were sent out from England by the Propagation Society, receiving a small stipend from it;
and thus was laid the foundation of the Church in
Canada in communion with that of England. In the

year 1791 an Act of Parliament was passed in England, authorizing the Crown to reserve certain portions of the waste lands belonging to the Crown, as they should be allotted, for the benefit of the Protestant Clergy. It was decided by the opinion of the judges in England, that these words were not confined to the Clergy of the Church of England, but embraced other Protestant denominations. These lands, consisting of large tracts of country, mixed up with lands allotted to settlers, waste and uncultivated, were a great inconvenience to the colonists. A portion of them was sold, and the proceeds invested in the funds in England and in Canada. In the year 1840 a stop was put to any further reservation of lands for the purpose, and the Roman Catholic clergy were admitted to a share of the funds; which then consisted partly of land, the greater portion of which was waste and uncultivated, and partly of the proceeds of the lands sold and invested, as I have said. The interest dividends and rents were paid to the Receiver-General of the province of Canada, and were to be applied by him, in pursuance of warrants to be from time to time issued by the Governor. The share payable to the Clergy of the Church of England was paid to the Propagation Society. In 1851 the Church of England Clergy received 12,000*l.*; the Presbyterians, 6,700*l.*; the United Synod of Presbyterians in Upper Canada, 464*l.*; the Roman Catholics, 1,369*l.*; and the Wesleyan Methodists, 639*l.* This property never was vested in the Bishops and Clergy of Canada; all they were entitled to was the payment of certain annual stipends out of it, to which the ministers of other religious bodies

LONDON :

GILBERT AND RIVINGTON, PRINTERS,

ST. JOHN'S SQUARE.

www.ingramcontent.com/pod-product-compliance
Lightning Source LLC
Chambersburg PA
CBHW031817090426
42739CB00008B/1311